Dear Marshall, Language Is Our Only Wilderness

Heather Sweeney

Spuyten Duyvil
New York City

© 2020 Heather Sweeney
ISBN 978-1-952419-26-3
Cover photo: Ian Costello

Library of Congress Cataloging-in-Publication Data

Names: Sweeney, Heather, author.
Title: Dear Marshall, language is our only wilderness / Heather Sweeney.
Description: New York City : Spuyten Duyvil, [2020] |
Identifiers: LCCN 2020028597 | ISBN 9781952419263 (paperback)
Classification: LCC PS3619.W442534 D43 2020 | DDC 818/.6--dc23
LC record available at https://lccn.loc.gov/2020028597

For Kurt, my love

*But I only wither to the earth, my personal
mess, and unable to utter a good word.*
—Frank O'Hara

Interlude: I am not on the syllabus. I am not from the hills or the vast ocean. I am peeled birch. I had gymnastics lessons. For a time. I was not hungry. The sun paraded for three months. I cannot tell you how much I love or do not love. I am things you cannot measure. I am not domestic. I ran track and was average. I always knew I would move somewhere far away. If I feel hemmed in I will retaliate. This is something to depend on.

Dear Marshall,
I went to Target today to buy a black mini skirt and had a feeling someone was following me. I calmed myself down, accusing my imagination. As I was paying I turned around and the guy was right behind me. Buying air fresheners. I remembered those boxing moves you taught me. My thoughts pinned under there. This is my world now. I imagine the sun rising across your voice. Across the flavored air. Are you at home now? At least that is something we could share.

I am not impressed by money although I do enjoy shopping and would spend my last dime on fashion rather than buy food. I like to run by the creek when it is slightly cool. I like the sun, but have had skin cancer. There is a tattoo of a sun on my ankle. I want to get *poet* on my inner wrist in intricate script so that when I am old I will remember who I am. As if that could save me. My grandmother had Alzheimer's. She was a nurse and smoked a pack of camels every day. She was also a gambler.

Dear Marshall,
It was the year of horses running through our bodies. Pause you who read this, and think for a moment of the long chain of iron, the first link of one memorable day. In summer school because we both flunked geometry. I threw the teacher's purse in the dumpster and never got caught. I don't know if you knew. Sometimes I think of you and then I'm like ok this is what it is and then I'm like ok, we are just the time everyone else forgot. Sometimes I feel a memory pulsing. Like when the field trip was cancelled. I never did go horseback riding. Sometimes I trace the shadow of an animal that is not there. Upon waking. But gently occurring. Leaning into a sharpening thought of you. Or I ignore the arresting color of a sunset. And stand in the light of a library window, opening the dictionary at random and landing upon the word, *bruise*.

I always told myself that I would have a housekeeper when I got older. I never dreamed of my wedding, although I did get married twice. I have never really cheated. My sexual drive is increasing. I got a Metallica tee shirt for my birthday this year. When I turned seven, I got an iron-on tee shirt that read, "foxy" and thought, it just cannot get any better than this. I wish I did not say "awesome" so much. I care less and less about what people think. I could not live without sight. My favorite place is the Tate Museum. I have been there exactly once. I am in love with color, but always wear black.

Dear Marshall,
I went bowling with my friends today. There is nothing like drinking beer at 2 p.m. on a Monday. I am either a gutter or a strike. I never miss. We never are. Complete. We never had enough time to.

I am having deja vu right now. I just found a seven of wands tarot card. It means speaking truth and also aggression. I laugh loudly. I get irritated by loud people. Sometimes I believe in crystals. I am sober today. My dog has a growth in his mouth and I hope it is not cancer. I live in two places. I love the smell of coffee in the morning. Starbucks is calling their coffee "rare and exotic." I see triple numbers all the time then I make a wish. If only I could have a wet dream. I want to be Holly Golightly for Halloween this year.

Dear Marshall,
I am lightly pressing the play button. I cannot help but think of us walking home from a party after that asshole jock was pawing at me and you stood between us. I left in a hurry and fell into some garbage cans on the way home through icy streets. You were two steps behind me. I cannot. It seems. The damp and the chill. On the inside. Can you see the seam of ice dividing my memories?

I am always cold. I lived in Arizona for a time and thought I would die. I eat out too much. I am allergic to red ants. I am living. After being bitten at an outdoor theater red welts and bumps expanded all over my body. The male nurse had longish blonde hair and was so nice. At that moment I decided that I prefer male nurses but still want female doctors. I try to be kind and sometimes fail. I love the mountains. I can lose track of time while hiking. Sometimes stray hairs fall down my blouse and I pick them out in public. I care about dogs. I dye my hair. My sister Shannon and I have the exact same notebooks. Rachel and I have the same shoes. We sang "Total Eclipse of the Heart" at karaoke.

Dear Marshall,
Your lyrics are a transparency between us.

My first boyfriend was a football player. Once, he lent me his Depeche Mode tee shirt. He had a mohawk and we watched 120 Minutes on MTV every weekend. I have been to a lot of concerts. The Cure was the most boring. I just saw Weezer in Del Mar on Labor Day. I don't like to smoke pot. It makes me paranoid. But sometimes things change. My favorite band is Belle and Sebastian. I don't take selfies. Any image of myself is a fantasy. I got locked out of my apartment today. I like to drink. I started drinking very young and once I start I cannot stop. After a while, I just stop caring. I can have great expectations for myself. I usually write poetry.

Dear Marshall,
No one can really start again. Let's go to the beach. Put the radio on. Fuck all this. When I hear your voice I want to party. Should I go to the bar or the gym tonight? I went for a walk by the creek. I am open. I am an heiress. You told me once. Ladybugs live in my hair. I am chain link. A thorn. Total trash. We live in a land of color now. Of fishnets and feathers. You are a subtle prism. You are part of my existence, part of myself. You have been in every line I have ever read. Recently, I went to a lecture on silence in literature. How to write absence. Time will tell. You are no monster. We were born with antlers. Or horns.

I am a market, a meadow, a bitch playing beer pong. This is how I do it. Bird of paradise on repeat. What can I touch? How many shots do you want? See the clots of soil under my dress. See the nape of the shore behind me. A stream of eucalyptus smoke. With a feather fallen in my sherbet. Flat champagne in the shower. Aqua Net on my tongue. A swan on the diving board. Plastic and teetering. I try to be pretty laid upon the stars. And, for effect, I have licked all the batteries. Now I am pressing my body to a window. A sheet of unfallen rain. What will prepare me for my next memory?

Dear Marshall,
You are subdued. And measured. And know how to keep friends. The night you stayed at my house when my parents were in Vegas. I still live by books. We are true ellipses. Barely touching. I loved you against. Reason. Against promise against peace against hope against happiness against all discouragement. That could be. We kept our clothes on all night. I came to you wild and you were a fucking gentleman.

Sometimes I am tired. I want to get back to. But I just wait. Untethered. It never feels quite like that time.

Dear Marshall,
Do you remember the lake? Or a summer night, jumping to the beat. In a forest or in a field. I didn't want to stop. I am a heightened rumor. The PTA is still gossiping about my promiscuity. I cannot contain myself. It is part of my genetics. I am a child. I am.

I am a breaking page. An aisle of live flamingos. I am becoming more and more. Remote. Driftwood and ash. My pearls are buried somewhere in the blinding skyline. The guy at 7-11 always hits on me when I buy cigarettes. He is about 60 and has a missing finger. I have to go teach my class.

Dear Marshall,
Please meet me in the iconic sunlight. Our words are never accurate enough. Check out my melody. Here we are shaped to become. We are e. none of the above. We are the bomb. A feral zone. The sky looks like a constellation of bruises today.

I pull the poem from a flat plain of wanting. Touching the soft fence of a dream. I am hammered down sequins. Anemic sunrise. A tube top on fire. Regression, a pale carnival. I hate to be land locked. I believe in touch, but this can be misread. I have been to a poetry reading at a laundromat. I am not a girl prodigy. I will not have sex in a limo or go to horse races. The last wine I drank was called dark horse. I will not ever be on television. I am slowly airbrushing my downfall.

Dear Marshall:
When we met I was graceless and you were full of haunting, a voltage I could not forget. Skipping school to drink a fifth of vodka in the alley. A horizontal icestorm between your teeth. Later that day, I don't know if I told you, I threw up at the dinner table. My dad called me a piece of trash as I fell to the floor. What can override our restlessness now?

I am an unspoken angle. Bent sky. I am damage or distance, I cannot decide which. Away from myself. I am cloud wound. I could. Yes. The erasure of bees upsets me. I can listen to NPR in small doses. I don't have a TV in Colorado. I used to want to be on The Real World. True story. My mom and I cried when Pablo died. I don't like desserts. I hate baby showers. I'm going to have a non-baby shower and register at Nordstrom. I'm going to have my cake. I've been through the jungle. I'm ready to kill.

Dear Marshall,
I thought of Puck when I saw someone walking a pit bull in my neighborhood this morning. I was near the corner of Adams and Idaho going into the liquor store. The guy said, "don't worry, he's friendly." I never worry about animals. So I pet that dog for a good minute before getting my wine. I'm still angry at your mom for putting her down.

I really like the sandwiches at that deli owned by a cult. I am having PMS right now. I'm horrible at poker. I was taught things too early. I have to paint my nails really dark. In winter I practiced roller skating in my basement. I hate show tunes. I can't wear yellow or pink. I had one cigarette today. Pardon me, four. These are the facts of life. I wanted to drink beer tonight, but had miso soup instead. I watched Richard Lewis stand-up earlier. I love men of all ages. I don't want to hold your baby. I like to run my fingers through cold sand.

Dear Marshall,
Years ago at your place in L.A. we traced ashes in your hot tub with swollen fingertips. We smoked. Drank red wine. Then. Your fingers became lit matches. We recalled firecrackers thrown at us by neighbor boys on bikes. To light soft matches through watery keyholes, a dream. Later, a seam of ash on my silky outfit. To taste your core then purest noise. Somewhere, an L.A. morning: the sunlit space between us, a kind of lesson. Splitting.

I think we will look back on all this the same way we do lobotomies. Hard core. I used to want to look like one of the girls in that Robert Palmer video. Black dress, red lipstick. I still want several days back. My friend Michelle is getting a hysterectomy today.

Dear Marshall,
Sometimes I remember us as a complete sentence. But this is seldom. I never told you that ten years ago, after I visited you, I was at a sushi restaurant in California and felt something slip out. I can barely write this as I made our way to the restroom in white linen pants and then returned to the table, announcing to my first husband that I did, in fact, want some sake. We will and do not speak of what fell out. We were already the fallen. More than once. It happened. But this is merely color and grammatical impression. When I went to visit you in L.A., I'm not sure if I ever mentioned, I told my husband I was going to a yoga retreat.

I am swept up by the condition of one note hovering in the car. Red mustang. A wave breaking my voice. Then residing. When there is nothing to reach for. I wait for the bell to have a cigarette as seagulls suture the sky. I am semi-natured. I look away and let it all pass. This may not be. This is the site of. A picture of this longing is on Instagram. A puncture.

Dear Marshall,
I want to be a devil for Halloween. Devil's night does not exist here in California. We were with my cousin Justin and his friends in the street lighting newspapers and plastic on fire. The old man across the street, panicked, waved his arms and ran after me. Hollowed breath. And then. I don't think I ever told you, but later an ambulance arrived. I told you later, maybe. But your reaction was not what I expected.

Last night I dreamed Rachel said *piendar deviantart* and wrote it in my notebook. We ate curry in the San Francisco underground. I woke up after sleeping ten hours. Today I am a wave of rust. Unwashed hours. A dirty palimpsest.

Dear Marshall,
I have not heard from Justin in many years. The last time I saw him I bailed him out for arson. I am ashamed to say I stole the money from Aunt Ellen who, if you recall, would say shitty things to me when my mom was out of earshot. "Honey you should hear what they say about you." But I would pretend to ignore her. It seems we tried to make ourselves invisible and then. Beneath winter. For a time. A mute flame. Sliding out from under us.

I am a taffeta cave, a tearless disco. I am blindly reaching for the center: blood show and dance floor. All I want is a little freedom. I am a salt lick among the planted mirrorballs. This is my unfinished animal. Painted backwards. This is how I believe in myself.

Dear Marshall,
I am listening to "Boys of Summer" even though you hate that song. Lost in the syntax of trees behind us. How can we start again? And become seaborn.

I am starting my period. And cutting my own bangs. This is called living the high life. I am crawling through the raindrops on your face. I want a beer. Tell me more about it. I used to have sex in cemeteries. That's what people say. I'm trying to draw clouds with my compact mirror, face up. It looks like a blurry constellation. It looks like a consequence of what I cannot say.

Dear Marshall,
What does the space between us demand? Please send me an x-ray of your voice. I am lying very still on this specimen slide. I have stopped watching the news. I saw a glimpse of you at the end of a movie the other day. Old footage. It took me by surprise. I am here, in lateral detail. I have tried to stop watching. Still, I cannot escape you. Piercing. I'm not sure what will unbreak us.

I am a glyph coming into the room. My diet coke says soulmate. I'm growing nails painted with exact words. With a thought threaded with rain. I arise molten and fractaled. Here. A foxy sty. A system. I am a hinge, a kind of waiting. An oar on your back. A didactical sunrise. I used to have panic attacks. This is the middle, regardless and always. I wear a lot of eyeliner. I am punctured by a small breeze. Look at the puddle in the sky. Keep looking. This is my pace my cheap my bad. My last bit of lip-gloss.

Dear Marshall,
You were always my witness. You never stopped me from myself. What does survival mean? A hand hidden. Under my coat. Despite my effort. Being chased by your mom's boyfriend with a broken beer bottle. Here, an abstraction. A hand that became a root piercing our shadow. When that fucker fell to the floor I swore I heard his tooth crack. And I laughed until I convulsed. When was the last time we. I invite you to touch my convulsion. My small empire of words. The bitch in me is this shattered frame. One day your eyes are blue and then another. Meet me in the hotel lobby tomorrow. I will be waiting. (Leopard coat, sunglasses.)

If a friend killed someone I would drive them around California until the cops caught up with us. I imagine this on the 101. The horizon is always beautiful but never actual. I want something I can touch. I love yellowing photographs. I have a photo of me and my sister outside with roller skates on and my brother on his big wheel. I'm wearing a tee shirt with a pig on it. My Chinese sign of the zodiac is a pig. I'm jealous of my sister's coat. Deep blue and embroidered, almost velvet.

Dear Marshall,
Between the river where. I find us. Did we ever touch the water. The swelling course of years. Rubbed raw with moments of lyric grafted onto us. That could determine. That could somehow save. The marsh of our words. In the terrible course of. I try to be tender. Tender nature. As if. All around me. All in words. My blue lips on your back, becoming a sentence. Settling somehow. Amidst the haze of. Flying ash. Amidst disaster.

There is a bee on my wrist. I am drinking almond milk chai. I know almond consumption is contributing to the drought in California, but I always forget. A bird hit my window this morning. My wingspan is five feet. I am good in an emergency. I am at a literary festival listening to a panel about the Middle East. Sometimes I feel dumb when it comes to politics. American culture, unraveling, worry beads, migration, Armenia, minorities, U2, strands, the tribe, millet, secular. I am losing ground. My attention span. I like to think of myself as a container. I will always go for broke. A broken modernity. I like CBS Sunday morning. I don't like to think about what progress means. I don't want to know what a century feels like.

Dear Marshall,
In Venice I thought of you, then also in terrible Germany. I wish we could meet in San Francisco at the MOMA again and talk about the books that make us cry. I told you. What do I deserve at this point? Can we go to Chinatown and shut that shit down then go to a strip club talking about the life we wanted? I wish you were. I cannot settle. Can we go to a café like normal people? I do not want to hurt us further but we are too open, too much of a pause, to ignore.

My feet are unusually narrow. I can run a long distance at a slow pace. I have had past-life visions. In one I am hunting a boar in a dense jungle. In another I am running with a baby in one arm wrapped in a brown blanket. We are close to death. In a field of ice. In the long neck of a dream.

Dear Marshall,
This is our next episode. We claim and we shed. Where is the break between us. Still, a stray ghost. A fume. As we become less and less. I'm all in. Ocean scribed. Watery, legible. I just want a sliver of our life to hold. I would settle for a hole. An icicle in my palm. A coarse hair fallen from skin. The unsaintly color of sky breathing between us.

I'm wearing a mala of bourbon and mange. You can see my black bra through my shirt. I look forward to sushi and sake later. This is a shaky timetable at best. I dream of the runway. And tailgate hours. My basin is flooded red. I am damned. I lick open an echo of grass. Upon. Someone's chest. I am leaving out the ladder. I am abbreviating my wreckage.

Dear Marshall,
I always expect to see you. Someone is yelling outside my window "I hate all you motherfuckers!" I want to tell you things in real time. Breathlessly. My scarf of clay. My shirt of ink. I'm waiting for the coffee to kick in. I recall the time our art class went to the museum and nothing bad happened. That day. We drew trees and arches. It was fall. A portrait of horses above the clouds. Then hot chocolate. Sometimes I think that was the best day of my life.

I am a sentence made of two icy twigs. Of splintered afterthought. I'm at the airport again. The wall of windows, a stanza. I cannot get this juice open. I have never touched a gun. I am a temple of blood and sleep. I know when to trust a stranger. When I see someone I want to fuck my ears burn and then my fingers shake. I'm standing in the street in dirty yoga pants waiting for the shuttle. A breeze against my calves. I am living through the slowest year on record. A child of want. There is sugar and there is heat. I'm having a cigarette. There is a sidewalk inside my mouth.

Dear Marshall,
I am your pause and your accident. Do you still have my copy of *A Coney Island of the Mind*? It was the first book of poetry I ever bought. I invite you to write into the margins. When we were both in San Francisco last weekend you didn't text me back. For some reason. You are across my entire life. I love then I am shattered. I hate and then I'm hollow.

I am plastic and academic. Present and tense. I am listening to Fiona Apple. I have too many daydreams. Here, the text becomes more like horses. I am trying to spread good things. Criminally. I am grinding the carcass of a bee with the coffee beans. I am a party in the window.

Dear Marshall,
These letters are a bandage for the shadow. You asthma and me anemia. I want to touch us evenly. In teacups of vodka. Wintered hue. A sugar cube crush. A single line on the floor of mirrors. Your mouth as a ledge. With a seam of white soot. I want to touch the dark circles sprouting under your eyes. Vowel-pressed. Fucked up. Shapeless. Can ever touch. Can ever.

I wake up with Dickens. In thickest light. Secreting my subtle. Craving pancakes. These days of bluest seed. My walk to the coffee shop. There is a rattle in my chest. I am angled toward the sea. I want to begin. Somehow. I went to the gym today and sat in the sauna. The end. I am a Tuesday of terrible hunger. On repeat. An unexcused absence. I have to get my shit together. Even though no one is watching.

Dear Marshall,
I have glimpsed our future and it is certain. We are a page of snow. Sometimes I just sit with the noise and play our names across the page. Our child is a velvet painting. I cannot stand myself as we. Sometimes trace and sometimes trance. The only time you left me at a party I woke up in a bathtub with something wet on my neck. In my hair. The missing blue vortex of your eyes, asunder. Dismembered ivy. Pulling me into a terrible wallpaper. I come open. Here, again.

I am a resort town for the apocalypse. I am wearing a zebra print thong. I love Modmarket. The endless iced tea. Sometimes I am a basic bitch. A morning of white rabbit and cold stones. I am a patient serpent song. Killing it. A crack in the cup. Wabi-sabi. A moth gliding through pink icing. I like to go to art galleries and pretend to be a collector. I wear heels and ask a lot of questions. Very softly.

Dear Marshall,
What can our emotions tell us about the ocean? And the names for seaweed down my shirt. May we live in the time birds awaken. Ever touching. Our frequency. Ever slipping out of the canyon. If anything, it becomes. Then it's all we have.

I am a failed reference, a fuckless night. Stars on a wire. I live inside a sentence of supposition. A phrase of bleached hair. A crossed out snowbank. Pulling ice from my paw. I write, go to class, teach. I am tempted. Then retouched. I am a child in paper weeds. The shape of hell between your teeth. A sorority girl throwing up in the back seat. Pull over. Unbuckle me. These words are rabbits where I kneel.

Dear Marshall,
It has been a while. I fade in and then. You know how it goes. I have to stop driving drunk. What happens when I leave too late. You remember. The party at your place. I still hate your manager. I told you he grabbed my ass as I left the bathroom and I threw my drink at him. That is why everything was shades of red that night and I could not. When you said nothing. Could not ever get over it.

I am thinning, an arching back. Against wings of velvet. I cannot handle myself. I cannot miss a beat. I am mangled and then a glittery glove. A tattoo of blue smoke around the neck. Craning.

Dear Marshall,
When you reach for my scenic heart of cellophane. I am loaded. Our words, buried in a Michigan sunset. Sometimes I fail and then. I think that this is what will take me down and then it doesn't. I just keep. Keep going.

I am a clot of seeds dissolving. Increasing winter. Sour. A pile of birds on the doorstep. Wreck and age. Unreadable partition. Shaken with rain. Across the shape of someone standing near you. The nearest stranger. This is how it works. I would. I like to listen to pop music at 2 am and write in a continuous stream into the feeling of not caring.

Dear Marshall,
You said I was fireproof but I do not agree. That nothing breaks. But you have not seen the leaves shaking in my body. You have not been to the show called my night terrors on ice. I don't know if I ever told you that when I moved to California there was an earthquake. I was pissing in the bathroom. I made my way through the small kitchen and hallway as the chandelier swayed like an inverted metronome. My husband and dog were already outside. I said, "What the fuck?" Laughing, he replied, "bros before hos."

I am dope and I am diamonds. I love a good dive bar. Now I am talking out of turn. Again. I am hundreds of miles away. This is a kind of race. I reject the order. I am an empty warehouse on fire. At the strand. Outdated. A strained dictation. Carbon leaves, a golden seagull. I am stain. Running toward a wall of mechanical wings. Out to sea. Ash on the keyboard. I hope these words do not return to me again.

Dear Marshall,
I am walking into a screen door with beer slipping down my tank top. Uncollected. A sharp moment. See the gravel between my words. See my tank top that reads hot shit. This is my insulation. I wish I had a phonograph. My homepage is a blister. I am on an airplane, middle seat, trying not to throw up.

I am the broken sun. A dirty receiver. The stale bread my lover brought over last night. Evidence of a past life. I am an unfamiliar bird stenciled on the most inner thigh.

Dear Marshall,
Come over. I'm burning things. And all the things we could not. Nothing was ever simple. Sometimes I appear human, believing only in birds.

I am forging my own signature as the grass becomes styrofoam. I wither to think of air strikes on hospitals and school shootings. Every day. I am a drone. I hover to glimpse our fragility. Crawling through the dust of my next memory. Find me drunk on the periphery and tell me everything is fine.

Dear Marshall,
You are my thesis statement. Summer keeps happening. In sharp petals. Let's go on a booze cruise and rip the sail to shreds. Under a pallid sun. Watching our gold stay. This is my sparrowed heart on display.

I am eating the afterbirth of the animal. Inside a red solo cup, the cheapest beer you ever had. My thighs stick to the chair. I am dirty crustacean. Succulent and swallowtail. A thin piece of paper. I am at a bar, photographing the light at the end of an overplayed song.

Dear Marshall,
I'm getting off the plane and writing my thesis. I am with my friend who said we should set an intention for the day. You would probably not like her. I have become an expert on turbulence and stealing drinks from the back of the airplane. I just sold a painting to a socialite. Your heart is my agent. I had to listen to her talk about her divorce. I felt ugly next to her. Sometimes I can be so mean. On the inside. But you already know. I just smiled and nodded like I do when someone is about to hand me money.

I am a dirty after hour. A shot of fireball held in the mouth too long. I am blackout and burden. I love to go to Target and look at the sale racks. I get a Snapple for the ride home. And buy animal bookends. There is nothing to touch here. Really. This is a latch to lick in the achy sunlight of the parking lot. I am refrain. Here my tongue is an anvil. Held to a metal horse.

Dear Marshall,
We could sit for a long time without talking. My punch card is full. It is nothing but holes now. Wind scrapes our skin. We are everything but. We are.

I am dragging ashes across my sheets. As a hand becomes a wave. Here to begin. I expect less than. There are words and weed on my floor. I am barely open anymore.

Dear Marshall,
Where does the river end? I look to you and think not. My timing is always terrible. Please forgive me. We are horrified saints.

I believe that everything gold can stay. There is icing coming out of my eyes. I have earned this. Even if no one else can. I will not follow. No one. I am not. I will not stand and kneel according to doctrine. There are colored eggshells cutting into my face. Accumulating.

Dear Marshall,
Let's watch *Easy Rider* again. I love that scene when you reach over and touch my shoulder. I am still collecting the anthem of stars falling from your face. I'm afraid we are both just demons now.

I am a bad holiday. Leftover wine in crystal glasses smashing the memory of a ribcage. Against fermented weather on the windowsill. There are dying branches on plates. There are wine stains on my notebook I decide to keep touching.

Dear Marshall,
I used to be your backup drinker, but now we have switched places. You are the wave I am biting at. I won't do and then I am everything. Below the foot of the Pacific Ocean.

I am swinging from a gold chain. I am stinger and I am sage. Between the dog's teeth, a cloud. I am a silent walk at midnight. I love to drive fast. That is how I roll. Sometimes. These are my reasons. This is my god.

Dear Marshall,
I am at Golden Gate Park. Writing letters. What is no longer definable? To carry this realm to rid. I withdraw the prophecy. You are my trigger warning. There is a family having a picnic next to me. Scooters and wine. This is the content of a long scratch. A shaky hole in the paper.

I am congregating in the aisle. Tearing at my shitty heart. I am a Starbucks logo floating on the tide below. I pull until everything becomes a pill rolling down. A terrible destiny. I just keep touching. The tiny tray, the arm rest. I'm dying right now because two women are arguing about where Utah is. Doing the crossword, window seat. I am an invisible landmark. I'm gonna lose my shit.

Dear Marshall,
I treasure the few moments between sleeping and waking when I forget that you exist.

I drop my head into confetti. I like to get fucked up. But just enough to. Delete a star. A spacing. I am driftwood. Retracing the sound. Falling out of me. I am pulled hair. Behind. I am suddenly, the smell of gasoline. Of unseen fire.

Dear Marshall,
I think of the times we went into the woods behind the trailer park. When our hands touch I don't care how cold we are. Anything is real. Again. Here, pulse and ice. Everwhere. Into woods. We were an unnamed season. A crown of crow wings. If anything your fingers laced through my hair. A crown of our own making. Leaves still stirring in my lap. And if we are the same then nothing.

I am trying to understand but that is the problem with me. I am trying to rock my own world. I have faith in attempting to write a complete sentence. Now I fall asleep with *Tropic of Cancer* between my thighs. No one ever. No one ever is enough. Or a sentence that belongs.

Dear Marshall,
I am at Ocean Beach. A shivering paraphrase. Watching a backwards wave. If I could touch the phrase at the back of your throat. The soft territory. I waver. There is German beer at the deli. At least. There is latent sunlight. Please ignore my last letter.

I am drawing animal heads into the newly born fog. I am almost home for no reason. Already blank, treading Pacific muscle. My nails are russian navy. Almost to one home now. To no one. Something smells funny in my apartment.

Dear Marshall,
Can we stand at the shore again as my sweater disintegrates under your hands. Please disrupt me. I get that sometimes you cannot handle me. I have heard that before. Regard me as a chapter of asymmetry. The cabbie who drove me to the airport was Australian. We talked about buffalo herds. Somehow. He made me laugh. Lost minutes among sharpest shell. I put my tears in the bottle that bore me. Recklessly, into the present.

I am borrowing from myself again. I want a drink and a cigarette the way some people want sunlight. I take nothing from no one. Truth is my angled centerpiece. Real love is ugly as fuck. A shard of light. I try to make it look pretty because what else can I do?

Dear Marshall,
I'm still making these shapes in the ocean of your shoulder where birds survive and still themselves at dawn. Inside your metallic dream sharpening into a fortress of flames. When waves break into sirens on our backs. Into a bank of carefully worded sand. Where I dissemble and hunger in your ruin.

I am so sick of myself. This beer is like water. I was misled. I am a calloused cloud. A veil of dirty ash. Everything I touch is. A vile pedagogy. These echoes suck. I know.

Dear Marshall,
A lot of time I am pretending now. Remember when nights were new on our fingers? Nothing could ever touch me more.

I am static. An imploding signifier. Standing in the way of myself. The brightness recovers. As a flame. My prayer of fire is easy. My prayer is an orgasm.

Dear Marshall,
You are a kind of punishment. A ghost of ferocity. Everything I write is a failed destiny. Do you remember that time your mom tried to get me to do crack with her. We were watching Wheel of Fortune. Am I still someone you used to know?

I am the cherry inside these rotting words. A cognac night of blemishes when the trees were brutal and armless. I am face down on the forest floor. The smallest hole going numb.

Dear Marshall,
My friend Tara visited me here in Boulder last week. We were high for six straight days. We made holiday cards and went hiking. She didn't ask about you. Not once.

I hate potlucks. Either have a party or don't. Here I lay as a broken blister. An imitation. This is where the waxy cups tremble. On a ledge of false arrogance. J'Lyn said this is not procedural. She is not sure what the procedure is though. This is where I self-medicate. Here the letters stop and try to change. To turn and face themselves.

Dear Marshall,
You are slowly learning that I have real feelings. I am scratching at the words I don't send you. Because. I falter. In some dimension of lilies. I am a different kind of grace now. Or ignorance. I am not sure anymore. Of anything.

I am bramble and gateway. Crusted with mud. I am not a role model or crying through an SPCA commercial. There is something like steel wool in my chest. There is a grammar of cocktail swords I am slowly sucking on.

Dear Marshall,
What are we made of? Cixous says it is our weaknesses. I have been taught to disagree with this. I feel that we are made of our scars. And that questions like this are slightly dangerous. That the truth has already been written as the enemy. But I can only exist here. Without you.

I am counting on one hand the things I fear anymore. I am a vial of blood worn as a pendant. The latitude of. Trying hard to be. I am in the ever-real. Ordering pot on amazon. Reaching the bottom of air itself. Reaching for a discontinued color.

Dear Marshall,
Is this the whole thing. I carry your meaning to erase. And again. I used to go to you, I mean go to yoga. Now I capture the cinders. As our legs subtly touch. Into a salted opening.

I am a peephole smeared with Vaseline. I kneel to catch ashes on my tongue. I am constantly asking myself if being friends with men is a myth. Of myself. This question, nailing me on a Sunday. If I ever could. If ever.

Dear Marshall,
I feel dangerously close to you even though we are separated by millions of rooftops. You can go to hell. I feel the sun as a postscript around our bodies. At someone's party where we didn't really belong. There were chandeliers and ice sculptures. There were stitches you got from the diving board accident and we cried all the way to the hospital. Your mom said the stitches were your graduation present. Sometimes I feel again and then sometimes it's like nothing ever was.

I am somewhere. I am. This will happen again. I am certain.

Dear Marshall,
Now I am someone's wife who makes jokes at parties about what a failure I am. Everyone laughs. I don't do home or dinner parties. I don't do all the things. That. I want you to wrap me in all the shades from a Hitchcock movie. In all that we ever saw.

I am slowly unwriting all of these sentences. Coastline tremors. Stuffed rabbits on the shelf. I put a stethoscope to fallen rain. I am a liquor store in a Midwestern field. The wine cooler that made you sick. I already thought. But this is all I knew. If only my dreams would trust themselves.

Dear Marshall,
Enter my pulse. Now the universe is ours.

I do not cry in public. Or private, usually. I decided this at a very young age. I can only do words now. This is a hunger for. And then hardened by. This reminds me of touching the sea. A restless sleep. Between everything.

Dear Marshall,
I am drinking cold coffee and writing comments on my friends' poems. Roger is writing about bitcoin and I have no fucking idea what that is. Last night we crawled through my dream. Together. Your finger across my mouth. Almost. Just as we are about to. I wake up and touch. Tell me you ache. The horizon would feel better then.

Maybe I deserve this failure. These feelings. My feelings are fluorescent. My feelings are playing on Spotify.

Dear Marshall,
I don't know what we are anymore. Sometimes I remember that we are two different people. True love was when you spit on the protestors in the parking lot of Planned Parenthood. And then the rainstorm settled into the bitter neon of the exit sign. Some have suggested I insert a climax here. I guess our indiscretions are not enough. Nothing ever is.

My family crest features three boars. I'm cold on all levels. A two-way blind spot. Rain settles on my array. Becoming my resin.

Dear Marshall,
Let's press our scars together again. What is it called when one person stops and the other keeps going? The truth will self-implode because now we call ourselves a different kind of tomorrow.

This meadow is pasted to my comeback. I am concrete. A mouth of moss. I come from players. Knots of rain record my delirium. My naked loop on display. Carving a flock into error. Tying me to the ankles of a rabbit.

Dear Marshall,
We were undressing each other in a pixilated snowstorm. I want you to lick the snow out of my clavicle to suck on the splinter of ice between my knees.

I am a fawn in the funnel. Willow in the airstream. Floating one decimal away from. There is something I cannot say. There is a circumference of birds I am naively running toward.

Dear Marshall,
Someone handed me a paper bag of baby teeth on the Bart. The other day. When I was another. When I woke up today I was water. And you were nothing. A mantle of air.

I am a winter morning, lofty and cinematic. Here. I am one syllable fallen through gauze. I am the time that time forgave me.

Dear Marshall,
Do you remember that part in *The Great Gatsby* when Daisy says she doesn't want to go home? Or maybe I am just making that up.

You can tell how shitty I feel about myself by how much make-up I am wearing. I am a bag of glitter thrown into a ditch. Hardly wishing for. Inside letters of wreckage. Inside anything.

Dear Marshall,
Maybe I will disgrace myself again today. Maybe the trick is to not expect anything. You are my filter. Last night I dreamt of pulling a plastic glove out of the corner of my right eye.

I always want to leave. I am capable of being alone. I am a camera facing the back of a crowd. I am at a literary festival in San Francisco. Someone just said be open to letting the world take you.

Dear Marshall,
Let's play cult leader. I'll let you hold the flowers this time. I'll be guns and you be roses.

Nature no longer completes me. I wake up and smell my own stem cells. Ragged and pacing. Sometimes tells me. Parts of me are useless now.

Dear Marshall,
Anthony Bourdain just killed a pig in Borneo and for some reason I thought of you.

I say I want everything and I mean it. I am still waiting on my tiara of live butterflies. Part of me believes it is possible. Part of me hangs from a wing, barely visible.

Dear Marshall,
We were bits of sky unfolding, holding hands for the camera. Prom night. We were drained. Inside a range of man-made stars. Passed out in someone's basement. Inside the reversal of rain.

A little drunk. I am all over town. In the worst way. I want to go swimming. My name is boundless affection. My name is candy fang. Touching the bluest vein you can find.

Dear Marshall,
I'm listening to Mos Def. It becomes my essay on lyrical prognosis. Where I will make us into naked scenery. Like a glacier on fire. And paint your aura. Into shades of us. Crushing.

I don't know what to say about change. Or control. I am not reliable.

Dear Marshall,
Your face gets me hard. Let's get high and order Thai food. And watch the clouds turn into each other. And then go to the races again. We placed our bets and always lost. But this is my turn now. This is the font our hooves left behind.

Sometimes I awaken as an altar. Of hooves and pig ears. Of a nest trampled by neon claws. Sometimes I pull away from myself. At dawn. When I am breastfeeding a piglet. Into a negative nativity scene.

Dear Marshall,
We are rabid sleep. I'm still holding your cigarette, dipping the smoke into honey. The city keeps going as I gather in the light between your fingers.

I want to. I am gentle. Then my heart becomes. A riot.

Dear Marshall,
I dreamt of the apocalypse last night. We survived.

Sometimes I hate myself and the wings of lava I have aborted. The knotted sea and the disquiet of my garbage. I am forgetting on purpose. I am listening to Hotel California. To the alignment that corrodes me.

Dear Marshall,
How are you? I left my cigarettes somewhere else last night. I am not a season you can live in right now. Even though the soul you don't think you have still haunts me. It is like a color you refuse to see.

Is this all the time we. I can go. On and on. Gone. Nothing ever is. A sunbreak of yellow leaves in my throat.

Dear Marshall,
armarshalldearmarshalldearmarshalldearmarshalldearmarshalldearmarshalldearmarshalldearmarshalldearmarshalldearmarshalldearmarshalldearmarshalldearmarshalldearmarshalldearmarshalldearmarshalldearmarsh

Unadorned, losing sleep. Prey to nothing. The highest crest upon. Imagine I was secretion. Of words. Lacquering myself until really seen.

Dear Marshall,
Please meet me at the stampede. This is the dirt in my mouth, the animal on your tongue. Language is our only wilderness. I believe, to behold now. Our book of bruises.

NOTES
(THE BORROWED, THE STOLEN, THE MODIFIED AND COMMODIFIED)

Page 5 contains my first obvious evidence of stolen material from Dickens' *Great Expectations*, although slightly changed: "Pause you who read this, and think for a moment of the long chain of iron of thorns of flowers. That would never bind you, but for the first link of one memorable day."

On page 7 I write about a growth in my dog's mouth. Dexter is totally fine.

On page 8 I write, "My sister Shannon and I have the same exact notebooks. Rachel and I have the same shoes." The notebooks I am referring to are called "Decomposition Books" and feature woodland animals on the cover who are all engaged in dialectical triangles. The shoes are black flats with pointed toes, from Target. (We painted our scuffs with black marker one night.)

On page 10 I say, "I loved you against. Reason against promise against peace against hope against happiness against all discouragement." Again, this is directly taken from *Great Expectations* with slight modifications, only in grammar.

On page 12 I say, "check out my melody" and this is directly stolen from the song "Hate it or Love it" by The Infamous West Coast. I heard this song upon viewing the movie *Straight Outta Compton*. It is epic.

On page 12 I also write that "The guy at 7-11 always hits on me when I go in to buy cigarettes." One time he gave me a lighter and said, "This is one way I can get closer to you."

On page 14 the lines, "I'm going to have my cake. I've been through the jungle. I'm ready to kill." are directly lifted from the documentary *Grey Gardens*. If have not seen this, you must.

On page 16 I say that "My friend Michelle is getting a hysterectomy today." This occurred due to complications from Essure. Do not get this birth control procedure. Bayer should be sued and taken down. Things are in the works.

On page 21 I write that "I wear a lot of eyeliner." This came to me after my 12 year old niece told me, "Your make-up is really harsh" on a family trip to Santa Fe.

I refer to a literary festival on page 23, which was the Jaipur Literary Festival in September of 2015 in Boulder, CO.

On page 27 I write that "I am trying to spread good things." This is borrowed from a slogan at the bottom of a Hope hummus container. I think the flavor was kale?

On page 32 the lines, "You said I was fireproof but I do not agree. That nothing breaks." are inspired by The National's song, "Fireproof." The lyrics are: "You're fireproof, nothing breaks your heart…"

On page 33 I say "I am dope and I am diamonds." This is plagiarized from the Lana Del Ray song "Money Power Glory."

On page 42 I write, "Tearing at my shitty heart." which is stolen from Rachel who drew a shaky heart in my notebook on the plane during turbulence on our way back from San Francisco and labeled it, "shitty heart."

On page 51 I paraphrase Helene Cixous from the book *Three Steps on the Ladder of Writing*. This may seem pretentious as fuck but I don't care. It is a great book.

On page 52 I include the phrase, "the ever-real" which is directly stolen from Jack Spicer's poem, "A Postscript to the Berkeley Renaissance."

I have a phrase, "the bottom of air itself," although I cannot remember where it is. That is also from a Jack Spicer poem. He is my new lover.

On page 56 I mention Roger writing about bitcoin. I kind of know what that is now.

On page 63 the literary festival I refer to is Litquake. It was Sara Mumolo who said, "Be open to letting the world take you."

As I finish these notes I am also painting my nails dark blue. The color is called "All In."

ACKNOWLEDGMENTS

I am beyond grateful to the following fellow writers and friends who were with me and supported me throughout the process: J'Lyn Chapman, Sara Veglahn, Rachel Parker Martin, Marie Conlan Krieter, Swanee Astrid Swanson, Angelica Barraza, Jenni Ashby, and Emily Clark.

I would like to thank Erin Slaughter and Lena Ziegler who gave an excerpt of *Dear Marshall* a very welcoming first home in *The Hunger Journal*.

A heartfelt thank you to my family: Shirley Sweeney, Terry Sweeney, Shannon EarthTree, Chris EarthTree, Didi EarthTree, Seann Sweeney, Kelle Sweeney, Kurt Lindemann, & our beloved Dexter.

HEATHER C SWEENEY, she/her, lives in San Diego where she writes, teaches and does visual art. She studied at Naropa University's Jack Kerouac School of Disembodied Poetics where she was the Allen Ginsberg Fellow. Her chapbooks include *Just Let Me Have This* (Selcouth Station Press) and *Same Bitch, Different Era: The Real Housewives Poems* (above/ground press). She is also the author of the collection, *Call Me California* (Finishing Line Press).